POLITICS ★ ★ TODAY

WHO ARE ★ POPULISTS

and What Do They Believe In?

Zachary Anderson

Cavendish Square

New York

Published in 2020 by Cavendish Square Publishing, LLC
243 5th Avenue, Suite 136, New York, NY 10016

Copyright © 2020 by Cavendish Square Publishing, LLC

First Edition

Cataloging-in-Publication Data

Names: Anderson, Zachary.
Title: Who are populists and what do they believe in? / Zachary Anderson.
Description: New York : Cavendish Square Publishing, 2020. | Series: Politics today | Includes glossary and index.
Identifiers: LCCN ISBN 9781502645180 (pbk.) | ISBN 9781502645197 (library bound) |ISBN 9781502645203 (ebook)
Subjects: LCSH: Populism--Juvenile literature. | United States--Politics and government--Juvenile literature.
Classification: LCC JC423.A536 2020 | DDC 320.56/62--dc23

Editorial Director: David McNamara
Editor: Lauren Wehner and Erin L. McCoy
Copy Editor: Nathan Heidelberger
Associate Art Director: Alan Sliwinski
Designer: Jessica Nevins
Production Coordinator: Karol Szymczuk
Photo Research: J8 Media

The photographs in this book are used by permission and through the courtesy of: Cover (left column- top to bottom) AXL/Shutterstock.com, Lane V. Erickson/Shutterstock.com, 3dfoto/Shutterstock.com, (right) Foto-select/Shutterstock; p. 4 Joseph Sohm/Shutterstock.com; p. 6 (left, right) Mark Wallheiser/Getty Images, Alex Wong/Getty Images; p. 9 Bill Wechter/AFP/Getty Images; p. 11 Nathaniel Currier/Wikimedia Commons/File:Boston Tea Party Currier colored.jpg/Public Domain; p. 13, 24 Bettmann/Getty Images; p. 14 Chip Somodevilla/Getty Images; p. 16 Emmanuel Dunand/AFP/Getty Images; p. 19 Everett Collection Inc/Alamy Stock Photo; p. 21 Library of Congress/Corbis/VCG/Getty Images; p. 23 US Army/Wikimedia Commons/File:101st Airborne at Little Rock Central High.jpg/Public Domain; p. 26 Shel Hershorn/Hulton Archive/Getty Images; p. 28 David McNew/Getty Images; p. 30 Ben Stansall/AFP/Getty Images; p. 34 Bill Clark/Roll Call/Getty Images; p. 36 Matt Cardy/Getty Images; p. 38 Stan Honda/AFP/Getty Images; p. 40 Alex Wong/Getty Images; p. 42 John Moore/Getty Images; p. 44 Luke Sharrett/Bloomberg/Getty Images; p. 45 Chip Somodevilla/Getty Images; p. 46 Chinatopix/AP Images.

Printed in the United States of America

★ Contents

Chapter 1

What Makes a Populist

The 2016 United States presidential election was extraordinary. As late as June 2016, with Election Day just months away, it still seemed possible that Senator Bernie Sanders of Vermont could overtake Secretary of State Hillary Clinton and win the Democratic Party's nomination. Meanwhile, Donald Trump, a reality TV star and business mogul with no experience in government, had already beaten a large field of challengers and won the Republican nomination.

Sanders and Trump could not have been more different politically. Sanders was calling for clean energy, free health care, and free college tuition. Trump demanded tax cuts, a wall along the US-Mexico border to prevent illegal immigration, and a ban on Muslims entering the country. Despite these differences, both were considered to be populists. How could two politicians with such radically different opinions both be populists? What is a populist, anyway?

Opposite: Supporters of Bernie Sanders cheer at a March 2016 rally. Sanders was one of two populist candidates who ran during the 2016 presidential election.

While Republican Donald Trump (*left*) and Democrat Bernie Sanders (*right*) campaigned on vastly different policy platforms in 2016, both were populists.

People vs. Power

When people think about politics, they often think in terms of policies or parties. A policy is a proposed action for the government to take, like making health care available for everyone or cutting taxes. Political parties are groups of people who share the same ideas about what policies they would like to see made into law. In the United States, the two most popular political parties are the Democratic Party and the Republican Party.

What makes populism unique as an ideology is that it can be found among the representatives of any political party and can be associated with any number of different policy ideas. That is why presidential candidates from different parties, such as Bernie Sanders and Donald Trump, can both be considered populists.

All of this may make it confusing to figure out whether or not a particular politician or political group is populist, but what makes someone populist is not the group they belong to or the goals they have. Instead, populism is about seeing the world as a fight between people and power.

A populist is someone who believes that society is basically divided into two groups. On one side is "the people." This group is made up of ordinary people from all walks of life—people such as coal miners and farmers, college students, and small-business owners. The other side controls economic or political power. This group is often called "the establishment," but it can have many different names, such as the "moneyed classes," "special interests," or "the elite." Just as this group can go by many names, the types of people who make up this powerful group can change over time. Sometimes it can be wealthy businesspeople and media moguls, and at other times it may be professional politicians or even people in foreign countries. Sometimes it can be a combination of all of these groups. To the populist, what makes the establishment different from the people is the way the establishment uses its power. A populist believes that the establishment is corrupt and uses its power to protect itself rather than to serve the people. In this sense, "populism" is just another word for any anti-establishment movement.

One helpful way to think about populism is to remember how President Abraham Lincoln defined good government. To him, democracy should be "of the people, by the people, and for the people." When people think the government (or any other powerful group) is no longer looking out for them, it is likely that a populist movement will rise up to challenge it.

Right-Wing vs. Left-Wing

Although a populist can hold almost any political belief, in the United States, there are two primary political ideologies, or ways of thinking, that lend themselves most often to populism. These are liberalism and conservatism. Liberals, who are popularly called the "left wing," generally believe that it is the government's responsibility to pass laws and regulations to protect citizens and help make society more equal. Conservatives, or the "right wing," believe that too much government actually hurts people and prevents them from exercising their freedoms and maximizing their potential. The terms "left wing" and "right wing" come from eighteenth-century France, when the two opposing groups in the government would sit at opposite sides of the room during their assembly—one on the left and the other on the right.

Of the two major political parties in the United States, the Democrats tend to be more liberal, while the Republicans tend to be more conservative. As of 2016, both parties had populist movements within their ranks. Among Democrats, Bernie Sanders led the left-wing populist movement during the presidential election. Donald Trump led a group of right-wing populists among Republicans.

Besides their different policy platforms, left-wing and right-wing populists distinguish themselves from one another in how they see the establishment and the people. According to journalist and political author John B. Judis, left-wing populists generally see the establishment as being directly against the interests of the people. In the case of Bernie Sanders's candidacy, he believed that a corrupt business establishment, made up of bankers, money managers, and other wealthy elites, had abused the financial system for their own gain. The situation peaked during the Great Recession beginning in 2007 and 2008, when the worst financial crisis in almost a century caused ordinary Americans' savings to dry up and home prices to plummet.

Right-wing populism, on the other hand, typically adds another group into this equation. To right-wing populists, the establishment corruptly favors one or more minority groups, usually to the detriment of the majority. This could be seen in

About five hundred Donald Trump supporters rallied in San Diego, California, in March 2017 as Trump visited prototypes of a border wall nearby.

Donald Trump's call for a wall to be built along the US-Mexico border to prevent illegal immigration. Here, the establishment is the federal, or national, government. Trump campaigned against an immigration policy that was commonly called "catch and release." Under this rule, government officers patrolling the border would capture migrants who were illegally crossing the border only to allow them to continue on into the country. To President Trump and his supporters, this policy unfairly protected migrants (the minority group) and hurt ordinary Americans (the people, or majority). They believed that migrants coming into the country illegally were taking jobs from Americans and, worse, committing violent crimes.

Talking Populism

One thing that makes it difficult to figure out what populism is, is that populist leaders and the people that follow them often won't call themselves populists. "Populist" can be considered a pejorative term, or a term with a negative meaning, because of populism's long and complicated history.

Regardless, it is possible to identify a populist based on the ways that he or she speaks. Because populists see the world a certain way, the way they describe the country's problems and their policies will likely include several buzzwords. For example, they may mention "the establishment" or "the elite" and the ways that those groups hurt "the people." They may complain about the "status quo" or "politics as usual" and offer solutions to help "ordinary Americans."

Take the following lines from Donald Trump's nomination speech at the 2016 Republican National Convention, for example:

> I will present the facts plainly and honestly. We cannot afford to be so politically correct anymore. So if you want to hear the corporate spin, the carefully crafted lies, and the media myths, the Democrats are holding their convention next week. But here, at our convention, there will be no lies. We will honor the American people with the truth, and nothing else.

In just this brief section, there are several keywords that signal Donald Trump's populist way of thinking. First of all, calling out and rejecting "political correctness" is common among more conservative populists like Trump. Political correctness is a way of speaking that is meant to be inoffensive toward certain groups of people, especially minority groups such as immigrants or people of color. To Trump and his supporters, though, the idea of political correctness restricts people's freedom to speak their mind. By rejecting politically correct language, Trump seeks to identify with the average American and suggests that he will restore their freedom to use language how they want.

From there, he starts to identify the establishment—corporations, the media, and Democrats—and the ways they abuse the people. That abuse, according to Trump, comes in the form of "spin," "myths," and "lies," all of which are meant to keep the people in the dark about what's really going on in the country. Instead, Trump says that he will be the one to speak the truth to the American people.

Roots of Populism in America

The word "populist" originated in the United States in the late nineteenth century. However, the history of populism in the United States stretches back even further, all the way to the country's founding. The American Revolution was, in many ways, a populist uprising. The early protests that sparked the revolution, such as the Boston Tea Party, were driven by colonists who were frustrated with the unfair actions of the British government.

After the colonies won independence from Great Britain, the Founding Fathers had to establish a new government. Among the problems they faced was figuring out how

The American Revolution can be thought of as a populist uprising, demonstrated by early popular protests such as the Boston Tea Party, shown here.

the government could better represent the interests of Americans, while still protecting the country from another revolution. When the Founding Fathers started to debate the laws of the new United States, they both respected and worried about the power of the people. They recognized that the people could cause just as much damage as a corrupt establishment such as the British Crown. History had shown that if the people were given too much power, it could lead to crime, rebellion, and mob rule.

When James Madison, who had been born to a prominent family of Virginia planters, was selected to draft the Constitution, he was especially sensitive to the risks of unchecked popular power. In one of a series of political pamphlets known as the Federalist Papers, he wrote:

> [Pure] democracies have ever been spectacles of turbulence and contention; have ever been found incompatible with personal security, or the rights of property; and have, in general, been as short in their lives as they have been violent in their deaths.

History had shown Madison that pure democracy was ineffective at best and dangerous at worst, and that the most popular decisions were not always the most prudent. He worried that the same chaos the United States had experienced during the revolution could be repeated again, and he concluded that laws were necessary to protect the people.

So, as Madison and the other Founding Fathers designed a new system of government, they took steps to constrain the people's power. When the Constitution was adopted in 1787, it allowed each state to decide who among its citizens could vote. In general, the franchise, or the group of people who can vote, was limited to a select group of Americans:

In 1787, the Founding Founders of the United States signed the Constitution.

white, landowning men. This was only a fraction of the US population as a whole. In fact, at the time George Washington was elected as the country's first president, only 6 percent of Americans could vote.

What's more, instead of allowing citizens to vote directly on every issue, the Constitution created a system of representational democracy, in which people would choose representatives, who in turn would cast their votes on the vast majority of key decisions and matters of law. These were the elected members of Congress. The input of ordinary citizens was further diluted by the fact that US senators were originally elected by state legislatures rather than by popular vote, until the Seventeenth Amendment put an end to this practice in 1913.

Although the right to vote has been greatly expanded since the founding of the United States, some checks on the people's power still exist today. When citizens vote in a presidential election, for example, the candidate who wins the majority of votes in a given state wins all of the votes of that state's Electoral College delegates (with very few exceptions). It is these delegates—not the voters themselves—who elect the president. That is why presidential election results distinguish between popular and electoral vote totals.

In November 2016, Donald Trump and his right-wing populist message proved victorious in the presidential election. The key to his victory was in winning what are called "swing" or "battleground" states. These are places where support for Republicans and Democrats is roughly equal, meaning that it is hard to predict what candidate these states will ultimately support. It is therefore these states that often swing an election toward one party's favor or another.

Despite losing the overall popular vote to Democratic candidate Hillary Clinton by nearly three million votes, Trump won a majority in swing states such as Wisconsin, Michigan, Ohio, Pennsylvania, and Florida, earning him enough electoral votes to win the election. He was the fifth president in history to win the electoral vote but lose the popular vote.

Trump's victory proved just how politically divided the United States had become. Demographic data collected by the Pew Research Foundation, a nonpartisan, not-for-profit

Donald Trump supporters rally for the Republican presidential candidate in Richmond, Virginia, on October 14, 2015.

research group, shows that 2016 voters sorted along strict racial, gender, and educational lines to a degree that hadn't been seen in recent years.

White voters preferred Trump to Clinton by 21 points, with Trump carrying 58 percent of the white vote to Clinton's 37 percent. Alternatively, Trump had little support among black and Hispanic voters, losing this group to Clinton by 80 percentage points (88 percent to 8 percent). A Trump-Clinton divide also existed between men and women. Men preferred Trump to Clinton by 12 points (53 percent to 41 percent), with almost the exact same number of women preferring Clinton (54 percent to 42 percent).

Just as remarkable was the support for Trump among non-college-educated voters. Those without a college degree were more likely to support Trump, who received votes from 52 percent of that group to Clinton's 44 percent, while those with a degree were more likely to support Clinton (52 percent to 43 percent). In fact, the less education a voter had received, the more likely they were to support Trump. This was the largest gap between college-educated and non-college-educated voters since the 1980 presidential election. This gap widened among non-college-educated white voters, with Trump carrying an incredible two-thirds (67 percent) of this group.

Taken together, this information paints a picture of the average Trump voter in 2016 as a white male with little or no college education. Pew research collected in March 2018 showed that those groups that had supported Trump during his candidacy continued to do so. Trump remained a figurehead for many conservative populists in the United States of 2019.

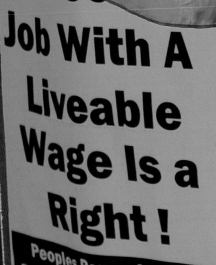

Chapter 2

Populists and Government

Populist movements commonly aim to effect change in government, since this is one of the most powerful establishments in a society. Democratic governments, as in the United States, are supposed to represent the interests of the people, but sometimes that is not the case.

Because populists can have any number of different political leanings, their approaches to how government can best represent the people can vary. When a populist movement sees businesses and corporations as being against the people, as the People's Party saw it in the late 1800s and early 1900s, they may ask for increased government assistance to help balance that inequality. However, other populist movements might see the government as unfairly interfering in their lives.

A New Movement

Movements that expressed populist thinking can be found throughout history, but the word "populist" did not exist until 1891. In May of that year, a group of Americans who

Opposite: On September 17, 2013, Occupy Wall Street protesters in New York commemorate the second anniversary of the movement.

had grown frustrated with the government coined the term to describe their new political views. The United States' first self-described populists were made up mostly of farmers and factory workers who felt that the wealthy were taking advantage of them. A drought in the 1880s had killed crops, leaving farmers on the verge of financial ruin. Meanwhile, these same family farmers were being slowly crowded out by large-scale corporate farming operations. These so-called "bonanza" farms could afford to undercut them on price because they employed cheap immigrant labor. Powerful railroad companies used their monopolies to charge higher and higher prices to ship farm products as well. Laborers who worked in factories faced long hours and dangerous working conditions while business owners collected huge profits, and wealthy banks squeezed both farmers and laborers with expensive loans.

Throughout the late 1800s, farmers and laborers began forming organizations with one another, such as the Knights of Labor and the Farmers' Alliance, to fight back against what they called "plutocracy," or a government run by the rich. As these organizations grew, they started to use their increasing voting power to pressure the government for protection against what they considered unfair corporate practices.

At first, the government ignored these calls for help. Although a deep political divide had contributed to the outbreak of the Civil War a few decades earlier, both political parties shared many of the same ideas. One of these ideas is called "laissez-faire." Laissez-faire is a French term meaning "let do." A laissez-faire ideology supports the belief that society, and especially the economy, functions best when people are left alone, and that government interference in economic matters only prevents the healthy competition between companies that makes the country prosperous.

Neither Democrats nor Republicans at the time thought it was their responsibility to tell the railroad companies how much they should charge or the factory owners how they should run their businesses. If a farmer or laborer was at risk of going broke or losing their property, that was their fault. As Julius Sterling Morton, President Grover Cleveland's secretary of agriculture from 1893 to 1897, put it, "The intelligent, practical, and successful farmer needs no aid from the government. The ignorant, impractical, and indolent [lazy] farmer deserves none."

The People's Party

When farmers and laborers realized that they could not influence government from the outside, they decided that they would form their own political party. In doing so, they hoped to challenge the government establishment and introduce new economic reforms that would better represent their needs. They called their group the People's Party.

The 1892 People's Party presidential ticket included James B. Weaver for president and James Field for vice president.

On July 4, 1892, the new party held a national convention in Omaha, Nebraska. Party members selected a candidate for president and agreed on their platform—the set of policies that candidates nominated by the party would advocate. These ideas were outlined in the Omaha Platform, which was written by a populist former congressman from Minnesota named Ignatius Donnelly. In the preamble, or introduction, to what became known as the "second Declaration of Independence," Donnelly wrote:

> We meet in the midst of a nation brought to the verge of moral, political, and material ruin. Corruption dominates the ballot-box, the Legislatures, the Congress, and touches even the … [judge's] bench. The people are demoralized … The fruits of the toil of millions are boldly stolen to build up colossal fortunes for a few …
>
> We seek to restore the government of the Republic to the hands of the "plain people," with whose class it originated … We believe that the powers of government—in other words, of the people—should be expanded … as rapidly and as far as the good sense of an intelligent people and the teachings of experience shall justify, to the end that oppression, injustice, and poverty shall eventually cease in the land.

The Omaha Platform had a number of populist ideas that were meant to help farmers and laborers. Much of the People's Party's policies were well ahead of their time. Although a few were just too radical to be adopted, like the proposal to abolish the railroad companies and hand over control of the rail lines to the government, many of their ideas eventually became law. For example, the People's Party was the first major national party to propose a civil service exam for government employees. However, perhaps most consequential of all was their proposal to create a graduated income tax, which taxes individuals based on their income, with those making more money (such as rich railroad tycoons and factory owners) paying a higher percentage of taxes. In 1913, the Sixteenth Amendment to the Constitution was ratified, making the collection of an income tax possible.

The Legacy of America's Populist Party

The People's Party had early success in elections around the country. In 1892, its presidential candidate carried 5 percent of the electoral vote and 8.5 percent of the popular vote. It was certainly not enough to win, but it showed that the party had significant support. It also had surprising success in the 1894 elections: People's Party candidates carried 10 percent of the country's overall vote, sending four congressmen and four senators to Washington, and another 465 representatives to state legislatures throughout the United States.

Despite these victories, the People's Party would prove to be short-lived. The Republican and Democratic Parties simply controlled too much of the political system for an independent third party to survive. Many People's Party members around the country abandoned their platform to support other candidates who had better odds at being elected. They figured it was better to compromise on some of their goals and have a candidate win than to stick to their guns and watch a candidate with populist leanings lose.

However, the 1892 and 1894 elections had shown Republicans and Democrats that the populists had a lot of support among voters, even if it wasn't enough to swing a presidential election. As a result, both parties moved toward compromising with the populists. In 1896, the Democrats nominated William Jennings Bryan for

William Jennings Bryan was the Democratic presidential candidate in 1896.

president. Bryan campaigned on a platform of regulating the railroad companies, minting more money to help poor farmers and laborers pay off loans, and restricting immigration to help laborers. That year, the People's Party chose to endorse Bryan rather than nominate its own candidate. This signaled the end of populism as the basis for an independent political party.

The Civil Rights Movement

Since the United States is a democracy, and citizens have a say in choosing their representatives based on their ideas, the country runs on majority rule. The government also protects its citizens' rights. But what happens when what the majority wants is to prevent those in the minority from exercising their freedom?

After the Civil War, Congress passed a series of constitutional amendments outlawing slavery and guaranteeing legal protections to all people, regardless of race. Black people, many of whom were once slaves, were now entitled to many of the same liberties as white people. Over the next few decades, however, white majorities passed laws, especially in Southern states, that discriminated against black people and restricted their freedom. These included so-called Jim Crow laws that prevented black people from voting. Other legislation allowed business owners to refuse service to black customers, and segregation laws made it illegal for black people to use the same public facilities as white people. Blacks were not allowed to attend the same schools, use the same restrooms, or even drink out of the same water fountains as whites. The national government officially condoned this discrimination in 1896, when the Supreme Court ruled in the case *Plessy v. Ferguson* that these "separate but equal" facilities were legal.

Federal troops escort black students into Little Rock Central High after the formerly all-white school was forced to desegregate in 1957.

Meanwhile, hate groups such as the Ku Klux Klan flourished. Black people suffered vandalism, assaults, and lynchings at the hands of these organizations, who rarely, if ever, faced any real consequences for their crimes.

In the 1950s and 1960s, black people started to organize to demand the same protection of their rights as white people had. This fight to end racial segregation and discrimination became known as the American civil rights movement. Under the leadership of such figures as Martin Luther King Jr. and Malcolm X, the civil rights movement pressured government to start protecting African Americans from unjust treatment and laws. In 1954, the Supreme Court ruled in *Brown v. Board of Education of Topeka* that "separate but equal" schools were no longer legal. Ten years later, in 1964, Congress passed the Civil Rights Act, which officially outlawed discrimination in public areas and in the workplace.

Joseph McCarthy and the Red Scare

At the same time that the civil rights movement was gaining steam, the United States was in the middle of the Cold War with the Soviet Union, also called the USSR. Instead of being fought directly on the battlefield, the Cold War was a tense political and diplomatic conflict between two different worldviews: democracy in the United States and communism in the USSR. In the United States, this conflict resulted in widespread paranoia about so-called "Reds" (those with allegiance to the red Soviet flag) living in the country.

The main leader during this Red Scare was Wisconsin senator Joseph McCarthy. He claimed that a corrupt

Senator Joseph McCarthy testifies to the US Senate about the alleged presence of communists within the State Department.

establishment made up of Soviet sympathizers had infiltrated the government to undermine the United States.

In February 1950, Senator McCarthy delivered his now-infamous "Enemies from Within" speech, where he held up a list of 205 names of people working in the government whom he accused of being communists. He claimed that they had enjoyed "all the benefits that the wealthiest Nation on earth has had to offer—the finest homes, the finest college education and the finest jobs in government we can give … The bright young men [in government] who are born with silver spoons in their mouths are the ones who have been most traitorous." McCarthy's populist and anti-elite rhetoric demanded that these and other Americans suspected of being communists be subjected to "loyalty tests" to root out Soviet sympathizers.

As a result of McCarthy's accusations, countless civilians and government employees were publicly investigated over their private political beliefs. According to one 1958 report, as many as 20 percent of American workers were forced to take some kind of loyalty test, in violation of their constitutional rights to free speech and association.

Over time, it became clear that McCarthy was using people's fears about communism to smear his political rivals. By 1954, McCarthy's support had vanished, and today, the populist movement he started is accepted to have been a "witch hunt," going after a perceived threat that didn't really exist.

George Wallace

The victories of the civil rights movement caused frustration among many whites, especially those in the South, who believed that the government was restricting their liberty. While laws such as the Civil Rights Act helped to protect minority rights, they also meant that white people were no longer allowed to discriminate against black people. In their mind, the government was suddenly interfering in their private lives and businesses, telling them how to hire their employees or forcing their children to attend certain schools.

This frustration eventually boiled over into a racist populist movement that was led by Governor George Wallace of Alabama. In his 1963 inaugural address, he called the national government's support for the civil rights movement a "tyranny that clanks its chains upon the South," and pledged to preserve "segregation now, segregation tomorrow, segregation forever." Later that year, he famously blocked the entrance to the University of Alabama, preventing two black students from entering.

In 1968, Wallace ran for president as part of the American Independent Party. He framed his platform as a fight against

Governor George Wallace blocks the entrance to the University of Alabama.

big government that was trampling on the rights of (white) citizens. On the television show *Meet the Press*, he said: "There's a backlash against big government in this country. This is a movement of the people … And I think that if the politicians get in the way a lot of them are going to get run over by this average man in the street." His message had broad support. In the election, Wallace won more than 9.9 million votes and forty-six electoral seats.

The Silent Majority

Wallace's candidacy had revealed something about the United States that would become an important trend in politics.

In 1976, a researcher named Donald Warren, who had been studying Wallace's campaign, found that a large part of his support came from what he called "middle American radicals," or "MARs." Warren wrote that this group of people was mostly made up of middle-class whites. What was most surprising was that they did not generally identify as either liberal or conservative. What united them was a feeling that they had been left behind by the country. While the rich grew richer and the poor and minorities received government assistance, these middle-class Americans felt like they were being forgotten.

MARs have played an important role in American politics ever since. During Richard Nixon's presidency, when protests against the Vietnam War sprang up across the country, Nixon brushed off his critics, saying that a "silent majority" still supported him. Ever since, populist leaders from Ronald Reagan to Donald Trump have claimed the support of the silent majority, with Trump once declaring, "The silent majority is back, and we're going to take our country back."

★ Chapter 3

Populists and the Economy

Populist movements in the United States have always been closely associated with the health of the economy. This is because ordinary people tend to worry about whether they can afford homes, find jobs, and pay their bills. Political polls frequently find that the economy tends to be among the most commonly mentioned issues for voters year after year.

In the twenty-first century, the United States suffered one of the worst financial crises in its history, the Great Recession, which also rippled across the world. As economic anxieties among Americans worsened, the recession gave birth to two unique populist movements: the Tea Party and the Occupy movement.

The Great Recession

Starting in 2007, the United States and global economies were struck by the worst financial crisis since the Great Depression of the 1930s. The crisis was marked by the longest period of joblessness and wealth loss in nearly a century. It came to be called the Great Recession.

Opposite: Demonstrators march in front of the Bank of Los Angeles in October 2011 to protest unfair business practices.

A Lehman Brothers employee carries a box of personal items after the major bank went bankrupt during the 2008 financial crash.

One of the primary causes of the Great Recession was the unchecked business practices of major financial institutions, such as banks and investment companies. Banks were offering loans for houses called subprime mortgages. These loans were called "subprime" because they were given to people who couldn't demonstrate that they could pay them back. This drove up the prices of homes beyond what they were actually worth, creating what economists call a "bubble." The homes, the investments they were built on, and a huge part of the global economy were at risk of "popping" like a bubble and losing all of their value. In 2007, the housing bubble did just that.

Almost overnight, people who had mortgages could no longer afford to pay them. Suddenly, the banks that had given out these mortgages were no longer getting paid. The housing market took a turn for the worse. There were suddenly too many houses for sale and no one to buy them. As a result, home values dropped by 30 percent.

The housing crisis was like the first in a line of dominoes, impacting every corner of the economy. People who kept their money in banks and investment portfolios suddenly rushed to withdraw it, and the stock market tumbled as hundreds of billions of dollars evaporated from the economy. For the next several years, the Great Recession would take a toll on not just the United States but the entire global financial system.

One common measure of the health of an economy is the unemployment rate. This is the percentage of people who don't have a job, are able to work, and are looking for a job. In October 2009, the US unemployment rate was nearly double what it had been a year earlier, with one in ten American workers—15 million people—unemployed. At the peak of the crisis, 8.5 million people lost their jobs.

The Great Recession created a perfect storm. As people lost their jobs and incomes, they struggled to pay their mortgages. But as home prices plummeted, people could not sell because they now owed more than their homes were worth. When people stopped paying their bills, banks that held the loans foreclosed on, or reclaimed, the properties. During the height of the Great Recession, approximately four million homes were foreclosed every year.

The Bank Bailouts

As ordinary people struggled to make ends meet, the US government took action in an attempt to help stabilize the economy. Beginning with George W. Bush's administration and continuing into Barack Obama's presidency, the federal government began passing bills to help contain the damage of the collapse and get the economy going again. On October 3, 2008, President Bush signed a law creating the Troubled Assets Relief Program (TARP), which allowed the federal government to buy $700 billion worth of debt from failing banks. Doing so helped keep local banks as well as major national banks such as Bank of America, Wells Fargo, Morgan Stanley, and Goldman Sachs from going bankrupt—and taking the life savings of Americans with them. These major banks were considered to be "too big to fail" because they played such an important role in the economy. If the government did not step in to save them, many believed the result would be catastrophic.

Americans began to feel a deep resentment toward the government and Wall Street. After all, the "bank bailouts," as they became known, most obviously helped bankers. While ordinary Americans were struggling to hang on to their jobs and homes, their tax dollars were going to benefit the very people responsible for the crisis in the first place. To make matters worse, many Wall Street banks that had received assistance from TARP continued to pay out bonuses to their executives and employees. A January 2009 report in the the *New York Times* found that the bank Goldman

Sachs had given 953 of its employees bonuses of $1 million or more. Altogether, $20 billion of taxpayer money went toward bank bonuses—that is, directly into bankers' pockets. The companies that had caused the problem had not only been saved from the consequences of their actions—they were profiting.

The Tea Party

As the economy slowly recovered from the crisis, anger at both Wall Street and Washington grew. This frustration split into two different populist movements, both motivated by the Great Recession and the government's response, but with very different aims. The first of these was the right-wing Tea Party movement, which first appeared in 2009.

The Tea Party took its name from the Boston Tea Party of more than two hundred years ago. The word "Tea" was an acronym, standing for "Taxed Enough Already." Throughout the housing crisis, the Tea Party protested the government's interference and accused it of propping up the big banks at taxpayer expense.

Later that year, President Obama moved toward accomplishing one of his major policies: expanding health insurance coverage. At the time, many Americans were covered by employer-provided insurance, while the elderly were covered by a government health-care plan called Medicare and low-income individuals were covered by Medicaid. However, this left a large part of the population uninsured. The Tea Party emerged as a major opponent of Obama's plan. Tea Partiers feared that health-care reform would increase their taxes and interfere with their access to health insurance. Just like the government's response to the Great Recession, the Tea Party believed health-care reform

A Tea Party supporter at the Taxpayer March on Washington in 2009 vents his frustration at government taxes.

threatened to support people who were lazy and undeserving at their expense.

Within the Tea Party was another, smaller populist group known as "Birthers." Birthers falsely claimed that Obama, who was born in Hawaii, was not an American citizen and therefore not eligible to be president. Among the most prominent voices in this movement was Donald Trump, who launched his political career by hiring investigators to look into President Obama's citizenship.

Occupy Wall Street

The other populist movement to grow out of the Great Recession was Occupy Wall Street, also called the Occupy movement. Like the Tea Party, the Occupy movement was outraged by the handling of the housing crisis. However, instead of blaming the government for intervening too much, as the Tea Party did, the Occupy movement believed that it did not go far enough.

By 2011, a few years after the worst of the Great Recession had passed, many Americans were still suffering from its effects. Homes remained unaffordable to many people, and jobs were still hard to come by. While bankers collected bonuses and investment managers earned huge profits, relief still had not come for ordinary Americans. It seemed that the wealthiest had grown too powerful and were using their enormous fortunes to influence politics in their favor.

In July 2011, an anti-corporate publication called *Adbusters* published a blog post advertising a massive, months-long protest to take place in New York City, the heart of the US financial system. They called on President Obama to "end the influence money has over our representatives in Washington" and declared, "It's time for Democracy Not Corporatocracy, we're doomed without it." After months of planning, the protest took place on September 17, when about one thousand protesters marched up and down Wall Street in New York's Financial District before settling in Zuccotti Park in lower Manhattan. Over the course of nearly

The financial crisis that rocked the United States in the late 2000s also affected countries around the world, but it especially affected members of the European Union (EU). In

"Vote Leave" supporters in Portsmouth, England, voice their support in 2016 for leaving the European Union.

the same way that the subprime mortgage crisis was caused by people who defaulted on their loans, certain EU nations that had been loaned money also defaulted. Suddenly, whole countries, including Greece, Ireland, Portugal, Spain, and Cyprus, were out of money, and they threatened to drag the whole EU down with them.

Just as in the United States, the financial crisis in the EU sparked a number of populist movements, both left-wing and right-wing. When other countries in the EU, especially Germany, agreed to bail out the countries that were at risk of going bankrupt, they instituted strict rules as a condition of their help. Countries such as Greece were required to raise taxes and roll back a large number of social-welfare programs. This heavily impacted ordinary Greek citizens, who were already facing hardship as a result of the crisis, and led to the rise in Greece of an extreme left-wing populist party called Syriza.

EU countries such as Germany and the United Kingdom (UK), which funded a large part of the bailouts, saw an opposite reaction. Anti-EU, right-wing populist movements sprang up. The most important of these eventually led to "Brexit," or the British exit from the EU. To many Britons, belonging to the EU tied them to a financial crisis for which they did not feel responsible. Leaving the EU seemed like an opportunity to take back control of their country. In June 2016, a majority of UK voters elected to leave. Two years later, the UK and EU continued to argue the terms of Britain's withdrawal.

Occupy protesters gather in One Police Plaza in New York City in September 2011 to oppose police brutality and big bank bailouts.

two months, the Occupy protesters lived in the park, using it as their base of operations. They built a tent city, collected and distributed donations, organized further protests, and even printed their own newspaper. Their efforts inspired dozens of similar movements around New York; throughout the country in places such as Boston, Chicago, and Los Angeles; and even around the world.

The Occupy movement's outrage centered primarily on economic inequality. The United States has some of the worst levels of economic inequality among developed countries. The movement's slogan, "We are the 99 percent," referenced a statistic claiming that the richest 1 percent of

Americans own between 30 to 40 percent of the country's overall wealth. Although it was designed to be a leaderless movement, Occupy protesters generally called for similar changes, including an end to corporate donations to political campaigns, increased regulations on banks and other financial firms, and more severe consequences for the companies and executives who had caused the Great Recession. A few years later, Bernie Sanders would run his presidential campaign on many of the same principles that inspired the Occupy movement.

★ Chapter 4

Populism Today

On November 8, 2016, Donald Trump won the US presidential election. His right-wing populist platform to "Make America Great Again" earned him majorities in enough states to carry the Electoral College. Since then, many of the policies he campaigned on have been made into law. As president, Donald Trump has had the opportunity to enact many populist policies and set the tone for populism both in the United States and around the world.

"America First"

In his January 2017 inauguration speech, Trump made the quintessential populist pledge to put America first. He said:

> We are transferring power from Washington, DC, and giving it back to you, the American People ... For too long, a small group in our nation's Capital has reaped the rewards of government while the people have borne the cost ... The establishment protected itself, but not the citizens of our country.

Opposite: President Donald Trump delivers his inaugural address on the steps of the Capitol on January 20, 2017.

Since taking office, President Trump has pursued policies that his populist base of support believes are crucial to the United States' national security, such as working to stop the flow of undocumented immigrants across the southern border. Trump's efforts to accomplish this goal have had a large impact on American society and politics.

Illegal immigration was among Trump's first and most important talking points. During his campaign, he famously pledged to construct a security wall along the US-Mexico border to stem the flow of immigrants, sparking chants of "Build that wall!" at many of his rallies. Congress has repeatedly denied Trump the funds to start his project, forcing him to turn to other strategies to stop undocumented aliens from entering the country.

In April 2018, President Trump's then–attorney general Jeff Sessions announced a policy of "zero tolerance" for illegal border crossings and authorized the separation of children from their families. In May, he made that policy even clearer: "If you are smuggling a child, then we will prosecute you and

A young girl from Central America sits on the thermal blanket provided to her at a US Border Patrol detention facility in McAllen, Texas, in 2014.

that child will be separated from you as required by law." The purpose of the policy, Sessions said, was specifically to deter, or prevent through punishment, illegal migration. As part of this policy, which had actually been going on for months, the government apprehended countless migrants and removed upwards of three thousand children from their parents, placing them in detention facilities that had been built at the border or with foster families. Reports of the extent of the government's family separation policy ignited public outcry, and protests sprang up around the country.

In December 2018, two children died while in custody, and many still had not been reunited with their parents.

Trade, Taxes, and Tariffs

In addition to taking action to restrict immigration, President Trump also has specific economic goals. He generally believes that the government is hurting US businesses. As a result of high taxes at home and unfair trade deals negotiated with countries abroad, American companies cannot compete with foreign companies. When Trump—himself a wealthy business owner—ran for president, he made tax cuts and tariffs on foreign goods major parts of his "Make America Great Again" platform.

In 2017, Congress passed the Tax Cuts and Jobs Act. In addition to instituting temporary cuts for families, the bill permanently slashed the amount of taxes paid by corporations from 35 percent to 21 percent. Trump and the Republicans argued that it would boost the American economy, encouraging businesses to use the money they would have spent on taxes to invest in their own growth and hire more people.

By October 2018, the economy was doing extremely well. The stock market hit record-high numbers and the

Populism in the Age of Automation

Donald Trump campaigned on the promise that he would bring manufacturing jobs back to the United States that had been lost as companies moved overseas. However, according to the US Federal Reserve, the government agency that acts as the central banking system for the whole country, the United States still manufactures a great deal. In fact, between 1980 and 2015, the amount of products made in America increased by over 150 percent. Over the same period, the number of workers employed in factories fell by nearly 50 percent. Where did all these manufacturing jobs go? It turns out that American factory workers *are* being replaced—not by foreign workers, but by robotic ones.

Robots like these, shown at a BMW assembly plant in South Carolina, have already started to displace human workers, possibly setting the stage for the next major populist movement.

This situation has led to the rise of a new type of populism, and its roots, are in one of the most elite, wealthy places in the United States: Silicon Valley. To these thinkers, it's not a matter of *if* artificial intelligence and robotics will replace humans in the workforce, but *when*. As the Federal Reserve shows, the march toward automation is already happening. By one estimate, as many as seventy million workers—a full third of the American workforce—will be replaced by robots by the year 2030.

In response to the growing threat automation poses to American workers, some in Washington, DC, and Silicon Valley, such as Tesla and SpaceX founder Elon Musk, are exploring the idea of a universal basic income, or UBI, as a way to support workers whose jobs are replaced by robots. A UBI would be like a welfare payment that would include enough money to cover the bare necessities—housing, food, clothing, and health-care costs—for everyone, whether they were employed or not. People could then choose to work in order to afford luxuries like entertainment or travel.

In some ways, supporters of UBI echo the People's Party from the 1800s, imagining a day when the wealth of the United States could finally lift all of the country's citizens out of poverty. It does have its opponents, however, who argue that a UBI could encourage people to be lazy, causing the economy to stall. Time will tell if technology will threaten the American worker and how the country will respond.

unemployment rate was at a historical low, at 3.9 percent. Trump took these statistics as proof of his bill's success. However, many economists worried that the

President Donald Trump signs the Tax Cuts and Jobs Act in December 2017.

economy would not grow enough to make up for the cost of the tax cuts. This, they argued, would increase the debt owed by the country and could lead to another economic downturn.

The stock market took a tumble at the end of the year, and 2018 became the worst year for stocks in a decade.

Trump also turned his attention to the trade deals the United States had made with other countries. He argued that deals such as the North American Free Trade Agreement (NAFTA) between the United States, Canada, and Mexico enabled foreign companies to undercut American businesses on price. US companies that could afford it were moving parts of their businesses overseas, while those that could not afford the move were forced to cut costs. As a result, ordinary American workers in industries from manufacturing to mining were faced with layoffs.

In order to correct what he saw as bad deals, Trump was aggressive in going after foreign businesses by implementing tariffs. A tariff is a tax that the government charges on foreign goods that are imported into the country. Tariffs help to protect domestic companies, or those that make products in a home country, because they make foreign goods more expensive. However, they can also spark what is called a "trade war," where countries begin charging each other higher and higher tariffs.

In January 2018, Trump began issuing billions of dollars' worth in tariffs on a number of countries'

A port in Qingdao, China, is piled with shipping containers in November 2018.

trade goods. In the following months, he began targeting China in particular. In response, the Chinese began issuing their own tariffs on American goods, especially on farm goods such as soybeans. By October 2018, those tariffs reached hundreds of billions of dollars, most of which was being paid for by American consumers.

Populism as a formal political ideology did not exist until the late 1800s, with the rise of the People's Party. Although these early populists' success was short-lived, populist movements have continued to flare up ever since. With the election of Donald Trump in the United States, Theresa May in the United Kingdom, Jair Bolsonaro in Brazil, and many other such leaders in democracies around the world, populist movements may be enjoying more success now than at any time in history. Though their individual policy goals may vary, their strategies remain the same: appealing to people's frustrations with the establishment—whether that's government, business, or, today, technology companies. As the world enters a new era fueled by populist anger and resentment, only time will tell if these new political movements will bring about positive change, cause lasting harm to society, or fizzle out like so many have before.

1891 A group of American farmers coin the term "populist" to describe their political views, which include opposition to unfair business practices and demands for increased government regulation.

1892 The People's Party nominates a presidential candidate and adopts the Omaha Platform, a formal set of policies meant to protect workers and small farmers.

1896 After a number of victories in previous elections, the People's Party endorses the presidential campaign of Democrat William Jennings Bryan, who runs on a platform that compromises with the populists. The move signals the end of the People's Party as an independent political party.

1950 Senator Joseph McCarthy rises to national prominence by capitalizing on people's fears about communism, launching a four-year campaign against alleged Soviet spies, lobbing countless baseless accusations against private American citizens, and smearing his political opponents.

1968 George Wallace runs for president on a racist populist platform that promises to reverse the gains made by the civil rights movement and reinstitute policies of racial segregation.

2007 The housing market collapses, kicking off the Great Recession.

2008 In October, President George W. Bush approves the Troubled Assets Relief Program (TARP). As a result of the "bank bailout," many major banks are saved, but taxpayer funds also go toward paying out bonuses to bank employees.

2009 The Tea Party movement organizes protests against big government around the country, the largest of which, the Taxpayer March on Washington, is held in September in Washington, DC.

2011 In March, Donald Trump makes his national political debut, announcing plans to run for president and falsely suggesting that then-president Barack Obama is not a US citizen.

2011 In September, protesters associated with the Occupy Wall Street movement camp in Zuccotti Park, at the heart of New York City's Financial District. They remain for a month and twenty-nine days and inspire similar anti-corporate protests around the world.

2015 Senator Bernie Sanders launches his presidential campaign, running on a left-wing populist platform inspired by the Occupy movement.

2016 In June, the "Brexit" movement in the United Kingdom elects to withdraw from the European Union.

2016 In July, Donald Trump wins the nomination for president at the Republican National Convention. Later that month, Hillary Clinton, a more establishment candidate, beats progressive populist Bernie Sanders for the Democratic nomination.

2016 In November, Donald Trump wins the presidential election in an upset.

2017 President Trump passes the Tax Cuts and Jobs Act.

2018 In January, President Trump begins to charge tariffs on a number of imports, especially on those coming from China. Other countries respond in kind, sparking a trade war.

2018 The Trump administration begins a "zero tolerance" immigration policy. Thousands of migrant children are separated from their families and put in detention centers, sparking public outcry.

America First Donald Trump's presidential campaign platform based on right-wing populist sentiment, calling for increased security along the US-Mexico border, a ban on immigrants from Muslim-majority countries, tax cuts, and tariffs on foreign imports.

conservatism A political ideology that, in the United States, believes in lower taxes, limited government regulation in business, and greater personal freedom.

Democratic Party The political party in the United States that tends to be more liberal, or left-wing.

demographic A group of people within a larger population.

elite A person or class of people with power or influence as a result of education or status.

establishment A controlling group.

franchise The group of people within a democratic society that can vote.

laissez-faire French for "let do," the belief that an economy functions best when it is free from interference or regulation by the government.

liberalism A political ideology that, in the United States, believes government can and should help reduce social inequalities, such as racial or economic inequality.

McCarthyism A right-wing populist movement in the United States during the Cold War named after Joseph McCarthy and characterized by suspicion and paranoia about Soviet infiltration in American society, especially in government.

mogul An important or powerful person, especially in the motion picture or media industry.

monopoly A business that enjoys exclusive control over a product or market.

Occupy movement A left-wing populist movement formed after the Great Recession that was critical of big business and called for increased taxes on the rich and greater government regulation of major banks and businesses.

party An organized political group that works together to advance their policies and candidates.

pejorative A word that has negative connotations.

platform A group of principles and policies that are adopted by a political party or candidate.

plutocracy Government by the rich; the idea that the wealthiest people within a society have an unfair amount of influence.

policy A plan for a government or political organization.

political correctness Speech that is meant to prevent offense.

populism A political ideology that believes an establishment, such as government, business, etc., is ignoring or actively working against the interests of "the people."

Republican Party The political party in the United States that tends to be more conservative, or right-wing.

segregation The policy of separating people of different races.

silent majority A political group made up of mostly white, middle-class, male Americans, who tend to vote more conservatively.

status quo The existing state of affairs.

swing state Also called a "battleground state," a US state where support for Democrats and Republicans is about equal and can therefore "swing" a presidential election toward one party's favor or another.

tariff A tax on foreign imports; tariffs are meant to raise the cost of foreign goods to encourage consumers to buy domestic goods instead.

Tea Party A right-wing populist movement formed after the Great Recession that was critical of big government and called for decreased taxes and government regulation.

undocumented immigrant Sometimes called an "illegal alien," a person who moves to a country without going through a regular immigration system.

unemployment rate The percentage of people who want a job but do not have one.

universal basic income (UBI) A populist welfare policy that would provide enough money to cover necessities, such as housing and food, regardless of employment status as a way of easing the effects of automation.

welfare Aid in the form of money or food that is given out, such as by the government, to people in need.

witch hunt The harassment and sometimes investigation into political opponents or those with unpopular views.

Books

Judis, John B. *The Populist Explosion: How the Great Recession Transformed American and European Politics.* New York: Columbia Global Reports, 2016.

Kazin, Michael. *The Populist Persuasion.* New York: HarperCollins, 1995.

Mudde, Cas, and Cristóbal Rovira Kaltwasser. *Populism: A Very Short Introduction.* New York: Oxford University Press, 2017.

Müller, Jan-Werner. *What Is Populism?* Philadephia: University of Pennsylvania Press, 2016.

Sunstein, Cass R. *#republic: Divided Democracy in the Age of Social Media.* Princeton, New Jersey: Princeton University Press, 2017.

Websites

BBC: Brexit
https://www.bbc.com/news/uk-politics-32810887
All the latest news on Brexit, or the British exit from the European Union, is gathered here by the BBC. This page explains the context and possible consequences of the Brexit vote and offers interesting demographic information and original infographics.

BBC: What Is Populism, and What Does the Term Actually Mean?
https://www.bbc.com/news/world-43301423
This helpful article from the BBC explains populism in general and takes a bird's-eye view of populist movements from around the world. It features photos, a video, and links to more news and information.

Encyclopaedia Britannica: The Populists
https://www.britannica.com/place/United-States/The-Populists
Encylopaedia Britannica's entry on the nineteenth-century
People's Party provides an in-depth look at the rise and fall
of the first true populist movement in the United States. It
features photos from the era and links to other topics in
American history.

Videos

Crash Course: Gilded Age Politics
https://www.youtube.com/watch?v=Spgdy3HkcSs
John Green hosts this entertaining and illuminating crash
course video on the Gilded Age, the era of US history that
sparked the world's first populist party, the People's Party.

The *Economist*: Populism Is Reshaping Our World
https://www.youtube.com/watch?v=ekc5EAPPPgk
This video produced by British newspaper the *Economist* looks
at the roots of modern populist movements from around the
world, from Italy to the United Kingdom to the United States.
Technological change is one of the major drivers of these
movements, and the *Economist* looks at how this affects ordinary
people and imagines how technology can actually help.

PBS: Divided States of America (Part 1)
https://www.pbs.org/video/frontline-divided-states-america
-night-one
This *Frontline* documentary explores the divisions in American
society that formed during Barack Obama's administration
and fueled Donald Trump's populist presidential campaign.

Bibliography

Bryan, Bob. "Republicans Have a Final Deal on Their Tax Bill—Here's What's in It." *Business Insider*, December 14, 2017. https://www.businessinsider.com/trump-gop-tax-reform-bill-details-corporate-tax-rate-brackets-2017-12.

Bump, Philip. "The Children Separated from Their Parents, by the Numbers." *Washington Post*, July 9, 2018. https://www.washingtonpost.com/news/politics/wp/2018/07/09/the-children-separated-from-their-parents-by-the-numbers/?noredirect=on&utm_ter m=.047e8109299a.

Cartledge, Paul. "The Democratic Experiment." BBC, February 17, 2011. http://www.bbc.co.uk/history/ancient/greeks/greekdemocracy_01.shtml.

Cassidy, John. "The Real Cost of the 2008 Financial Crisis." *New Yorker*, September 17, 2018. https://www.newyorker.com/magazine/2018/09/17/the-real-cost-of-the-2008-financial-crisis.

Chappell, Bill. "Occupy Wall Street: From a Blog Post to a Movement." NPR, October 20, 2011. https://www.npr.org/2011/10/20/141530025/occupy-wall-street-from-a-blog-post-to-a-movement.

Cunningham, Evan. "Great Recession, Great Recovery? Trends from the Current Population Survey." US Bureau of Labor Statistics, April 2018. https://www.bls.gov/opub/mlr/2018/article/great-recession-great-recovery.htm.

Fandos, Nicholas. "Donald Trump Defiantly Rallies a New 'Silent Majority' in a Visit to Arizona." *New York Times*, July 11, 2015. https://www.nytimes.com/2015/07/12/us/politics/donald-trump-defiantly-rallies-a-new-silent-majority-in-a-visit-to-arizona.html.

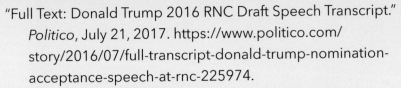

"Full Text: Donald Trump 2016 RNC Draft Speech Transcript."
   Politico, July 21, 2017. https://www.politico.com/
   story/2016/07/full-transcript-donald-trump-nomination-
   acceptance-speech-at-rnc-225974.

Gale, William G., Hilary Gelfond, Aaron Krupkin, Mark J.
   Mazur, and Eric Toder. "Effects of the Tax Cuts and Jobs
   Act: A Preliminary Analysis." Tax Policy Center, June
   13, 2018. https://www.brookings.edu/wp-content/
   uploads/2018/06/ES_20180608_tcja_summary_paper_
   final.pdf.

Gautney, Heather. "What Is Occupy Wall Street? The History
   of Leaderless Movements." *Washington Post*, October
   10, 2011. https://www.washingtonpost.com/national/
   on-leadership/what-is-occupy-wall-street-the-history-of-
   leaderless-movements/2011/10/10/gIQAwkFjaL_story.
   html?noredirect=on&utm_term=.3b971beaafa5.

Goodhart, David. *The Road to Somewhere: The Populist Revolt
   and the Future of Politics*. New York: Oxford University
   Press, 2017.

"The Great Recession: Over but Not Gone?" Northwestern
   University, 2014. https://www.ipr.northwestern.edu/about/
   news/2014/IPR-research-Great-Recession-unemployment-
   foreclosures-safety-net-fertility-public-opinion.html.

"Have You No Sense of Decency?" US Senate, June 9, 1954.
   https://www.senate.gov/artandhistory/history/minute/
   Have_you_no_sense_of_decency.htm.

"Inaugural Address of Governor George Wallace, Which
   Was Delivered at the Capitol in Montgomery, Alabama."
   Alabama Department of Archives and History, January
   14, 1963. http://digital.archives.alabama.gov/cdm/ref/
   collection/voices/id/2952.

Isidore, Chris. "2018 Was the Worst for Stocks in 10 Years."
CNN Business, December 31, 2018. https://www.cnn.
com/2018/12/31/investing/dow-stock-market-today/
index.html.

Ito, Joi. "The Paradox of Universal Basic Income." *Wired*,
March 29, 2018. https://www.wired.com/story/the-
paradox-of-universal-basic-income.

Judis, John B. *The Populist Explosion: How the Great
Recession Transformed American and European Politics.*
New York: Columbia Global Reports, 2016.

Kakutani, Michiko. *The Death of Truth: Notes on Falsehood in
the Age of Trump.* New York: Tim Duggan Books, 2018.

Kazin, Michael. *The Populist Persuasion.* New York:
HarperCollins, 1995.

Lepore, Jill. "Rock, Paper, Scissors: How We Used to Vote."
New Yorker, October 13, 2008. https://www.newyorker.
com/magazine/2008/10/13/rock-paper-scissors.

Madison, James. "The Federalist Papers: No. 10." Yale Law
School, November 23, 1787. http://avalon.law.yale.
edu/18th_century/fed10.asp.

McCarthy, Joseph. "Enemies from Within." George Mason
University, February 9, 1950. http://historymatters.gmu.
edu/d/6456.

"Occupy Wall Street Timelines." *Rolling Stone*, October
18, 2011. https://www.rollingstone.com/politics/
politics-lists/occupy-wall-street-timeline-18147/
september-20-2011-177489.

"The Omaha Platform: Launching the Populist Party." George
Mason University. Accessed September 27, 2018. http://
historymatters.gmu.edu/d/5361.

Paquette, Danielle. "Robots Could Replace Nearly a Third of the U.S. Workforce by 2030." *Washington Post*, November 30, 2017. https://www.washingtonpost.com/news/wonk/wp/2017/11/30/robots-could-soon-replace-nearly-a-third-of-the-u-s-workforce/?noredirect=on&utm_term=.4808329dcc5e.

Rosen, Jeffrey. "America Is Living James Madison's Nightmare." *Atlantic*, September 18, 2018. https://www.theatlantic.com/magazine/archive/2018/10/james-madison-mob-rule/568351/?utm_source=nextdraft&utm_medium=email.

Schwartz, Nelson D. "The Recovery Threw the Middle-Class Dream Under a Benz." *New York Times*, September 12, 2018. https://www.nytimes.com/2018/09/12/business/middle-class-financial-crisis.html.

Sessions, Jefferson Beauregard, III. "Attorney General Sessions Delivers Remarks Discussing the Immigration Enforcement Actions of the Trump Administration." US Department of Justice, May 7, 2018. https://www.justice.gov/opa/speech/attorney-general-sessions-delivers-remarks-discussing-immigration-enforcement-actions.

Snyder, Timothy. *The Road to Unfreedom*. New York: Tim Duggan Books, 2018.

Sorkin, Andrew Ross. "From Trump to Trade, the Financial Crisis Still Resonates 10 Years Later." *New York Times*, September 10, 2018. https://www.nytimes.com/2018/09/10/business/dealbook/financial-crisis-trump.html.

Storrs, Landon R. Y. "McCarthyism and the Second Red
Scare." Oxford Research Encyclopedias, July 2015.
http://americanhistory.oxfordre.com/view/10.1093/
acrefore/9780199329175.001.0001/acrefore-
9780199329175-e-6.

Story, Louise and Eric Dash. "Bankers Reaped Lavish Bonuses
During Bailouts." *New York Times*, July 30, 2009. https://
www.nytimes.com/2009/07/31/business/31pay.html.

Sunstein, Cass R. *#republic: Divided Democracy in the Age
of Social Media*. Princeton, NJ: Princeton University Press,
2017.

Swanson, Ana. "A Single Chart Everybody Needs to Look at
Before Trump's Big Fight over Bringing Back American
Jobs." *Washington Post*, November 28, 2016. https://
www.washingtonpost.com/news/wonk/wp/2016/11/28/
theres-a-big-reason-trump-might-not-be-able-to-
keep-his-promise-on-jobs/?noredirect=on&utm_
term=.31b27710f2d3.

"TARP Programs." US Department of the Treasury. Accessed
September 27, 2018. https://www.treasury.gov/initiatives/
financial-stability/TARP-Programs/Pages/default.aspx#.

Terrell, Ellen. "History of the US Income Tax." Library of
Congress, 2012. https://www.loc.gov/rr/business/
hottopic/irs_history.html.

Trump, Donald. "The Inaugural Address." WhiteHouse.gov,
January 20, 2017. https://www.whitehouse.gov/briefings-
statements/the-inaugural-address.

"2016 Presidential Election." 270 to Win. Accessed September
27, 2018. https://www.270towin.com/2016_Election.

Tyson, Alec, and Shiva Maniam. "Behind Trump's Victory, Divisions by Race, Gender, Education." Pew Research Center, November 9, 2016. http://www.pewresearch.org/fact-tank/2016/11/09/behind-trumps-victory-divisions-by-race-gender-education.

"Wide Differences in Trump Approval by Race, Education, Religious Affiliation." Pew Research Center, March 15, 2018. http://www.pewresearch.org/fact-tank/2018/03/15/disagreements-about-trump-widely-seen-as-reflecting-divides-over-other-values-and-goals/ft_18-03-15_trumpvalues_demographic.

Index

Page numbers in **boldface** refer to images.

Zachary Anderson is a freelance writer with degrees in political science and English. In addition to writing, he enjoys watching political debates, volunteering to sign up new voters, and hiking in the Adirondacks. He lives in New York with his wife and daughter.